Disasters *in* Nature

Volcanoes

Catherine Chambers

Heinemann
LIBRARY

www.heinemann.co.uk
Visit our website to find out more information about Heinemann Library books.

To order:
 Phone 44 (0) 1865 888066
 Send a fax to 44 (0) 1865 314091
 Visit the Heinemann Bookshop at www.heinemann.co.uk to browse our catalogue and order online.

First published in Great Britain by Heinemann Library, Halley Court, Jordan Hill, Oxford OX2 8EJ
a division of Reed Educational and Professional Publishing Ltd. Heinemann is a registered trademark of Reed Educational & Professional Publishing Ltd.

OXFORD MELBOURNE AUCKLAND JOHANNESBURG BLANTYRE
GABORONE IBADAN PORTSMOUTH (NH) USA CHICAGO

Designed by Celia Floyd
Orginated by Dot Gradatons
Printed by Wing King Tong in Hong Kong

ISBN 0 431 09601 5 (hardback)
03 02 01 00
10 9 8 7 6 5 4 3 2 1

ISBN 0 431 09608 2 (paperback)
03 02 01 00
10 9 8 7 6 5 4 3 2 1

British Library Cataloguing in Publication Data

Chambers, Catherine
  Volcano. – (Disasters in Nature)
  1. Volcanoes – Juvenile literature
  I. Title
  551.2'1

Acknowledgements

The Publishers would like to thank the following for permission to reproduce photographs:

BBC Natural History Unit: Georgette Douwman pg.41, Michael Pitts pg.20; *Bruce Coleman Collection*: Charlie Ott pg.25; *Corbis*: pg.37, Peter Turnley pg.22; *Dennis Flaherty*: pg.37; *Environmental Images*: Phil Harris pg.31; *FLPA*: M Zhilin pg.24, Panda/G Tomarchio pg.32, S Jonasson pg.16, pg.33, USDA Forest Service pg.11; *Katz Pictures*: Donatello Brogioni pg.11; *Oxford Scientific Films*: Dieter & Mary Plage pg.27; *Panos*: Chris Stowers pg.23, Rob Huibers pg.7, pg.9, pg.34; *Photri*: pg.35; *Pictor*: pg.43; *Planet Earth Picture*: Bourseiller & Durieux pg.29, pg.42, Durieux pg.6, John Lythgoe pg.21, Krafft pg.5, pg.17, pg.39, Richard Coomber pg.45.

Cover photograph reproduced with permission of Still Pictures.

Our thanks to Mandy Barker for her comments in the preparation of this book.

Every effort has been made to contact copyright holders of any material reproduced in this book. Any omissions will be rectified in subsequent printings if notice is given to the Publisher.

Any words appearing in the text in bold, **like this**, are explained in the Glossary.

Contents

Introduction

What is a volcano?	4
Montserrat	6
After the disaster	8
Hitting the headlines	10

The volcano furnace

Where and how?	12
Inside a volcano	14
Making volcano shapes	16
Erratic eruptions	18
Lava land	20

Dangers to the Earth

Gas, acid and ash	22
Affecting the weather	24
Rumbling Earth – raging waves	26

Watching the volcano

Taking the pulse	28
Watching water	30
Preventing the damage	32

Living in danger

Victims of volcanoes	34
Why live in danger?	36
Hot water	38
Life on Earth	40
Volcanoes in history	42
Amazing volcanoes	44
Glossary	46
Index	48

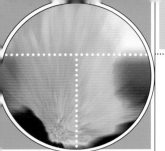

What is a volcano?

A volcano is an eruption of ash, gases and molten rock from below the Earth's crust. The deadly substances spurt or ooze through cracks and faults, up into the sky and over the land. As they cool, the **lava** and ashes form new landscapes. A volcanic cone rises above the ground, with a deep, empty **crater** at the centre where lava, gas and ash once pushed through.

None of these amazing volcanic features occur, however, without some destruction of the natural world around them. Frequently there is loss of human life. A huge volcanic eruption is nearly always a natural disaster.

Volcanoes are a devastating form of natural disaster. This is a night-time eruption of a volcano on the island of Reunion in the Indian Ocean.

Where do volcanoes happen?

Extinct volcanoes can be found all over the world, their shapes worn down over time. Most active volcanoes have formed where the Earth's crust is fractured by massive ridges and troughs that cut across ocean beds and dry land. The map on page 5 shows where they are. These fractures are moving all the time, causing pressure on the layer of sticky, molten rock that lies beneath the Earth's surface. When the hot rock gets pushed up through these cracks, a volcano erupts.

Volcanoes in our hands

Some volcanoes appear to be dead, some seem to be **dormant** (sleeping) and some are active in a small way all the time. All these volcanoes concern the people living near them, but no one, not even **vulcanologists** (scientists who study volcanoes), can be certain that a volcano is safe. Some erupt after lying dormant for thousands of years. This makes it very difficult to predict volcanic eruptions. However, archaeological evidence and remains are preserved in the hot lava flow and ash. This has helped scientists not only to predict what might happen to those volcanoes in future eruptions, but also to paint an accurate picture of life long ago in areas close to volcanoes.

Volcanoes on our minds

With global satellite communications we can follow the story of an active volcano as it unfolds – from the first puffs of smoke to the final burst of gas, ash and lava. Long ago, no one knew about volcanic eruptions if they happened on the other side of the world, but eyewitness accounts show that people observed very closely volcanoes that erupted near to them.

This map shows where most of the world's active volcanoes are – so far as we can tell.

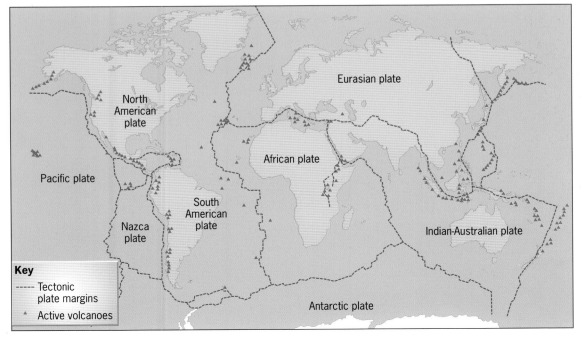

Key
- - - - - Tectonic plate margins
▲ Active volcanoes

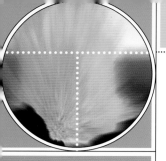

Montserrat

Montserrat, a British territory in the Caribbean, and often called the Emerald Isle, was once a small, thriving island. It now lies deserted. Its capital city has disappeared and the once lush vegetation is covered in ash.

The giant wakes

The volcanic Soufriere Hills had been **dormant** for 100 years, but in July 1995 steam and gas emerged from small, high **vents** – one of the first signs of volcanic activity. Within a few days, the explosions began and scientists warned that 'the big one' would erupt sooner or later. People prepared for the worst. Farmers began to harvest their crops quickly and moved their animals to safety. As a heavy shower of ash covered the capital, Plymouth, the inhabitants were advised to **evacuate**.

Many of the island's 11 000 people, who occupied the southern half, moved to the north. They waited for the worst to pass – but it didn't. The whole south of the island turned grey as ash smothered everything in sight. Montserrat's economy, based on agriculture, was ruined. Over half the population left the island altogether.

As the volcano on Monserrat continued rumbling and erupting, a new **delta** of land was built out into the sea from **lava** and ash flows.

A year after the volcano awoke it still showed no sign of going back to sleep. Its top swelled into two **domes** which eventually collapsed. A lava flow swept down the steep valleys and into the ocean and a new delta of land was created. By 2 December 1996, **vulcanologists** predicted that the volcano would throw out 350 million tonnes of ash and rock. It had already erupted 60 million tonnes in the week before the prediction. The British **Geological** Survey team and a top US vulcanologist watched the situation closely.

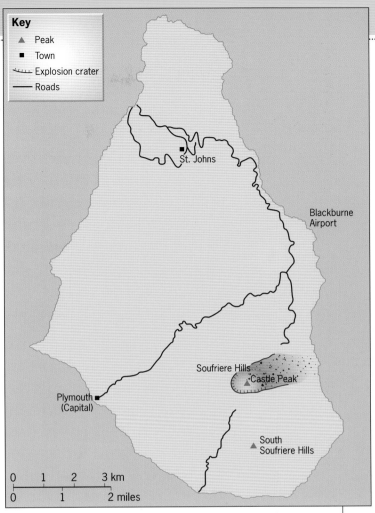

The Caribbean island of Monserrat.

The giant roars

In May 1997, superheated ash, rock and gas spat thousands of metres into the air, and the alert level was raised from amber to orange – just two colours away from the highest warning. The Montserrat Volcano Observatory cautioned that more people would have to evacuate the island – especially the 120 who remained in high-risk areas in the centre and south.

In June, bigger eruptions rocked the island. And on 25 June, **pyroclastic flows** shot in all directions at over 200 kilometres per hour (about 125 miles per hour), smothering villages. Twenty people were killed – the first casualties recorded. The south finally became totally uninhabitable and everyone left the island. In August, more eruptions gushed from the Soufriere Hills, and it has been spitting and oozing ever since.

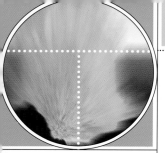

After the disaster

What have we learned?

Montserrat taught scientists a lot about the formation of volcanoes as they watched the first of two new volcanic **domes** grow. It began in September 1995 as a small tube of sticky **lava** rising inside the **crater**. This type of lava is called **andesite**. It is rather like thick treacle and oozes out slowly, cooling into a lump. As more lava appears and oozes over the top, layers cover the lump and harden until it grows into a dome.

As it grows, the dome stops more lava from coming out of the crater. It presses against the old volcano walls as it expands. This is exactly what happened in Montserrat. The dome became more and more dangerous as it grew until, in September 1996, the pressure forced landslides of hard lava and rock from the old volcano walls. This pressure also caused the violent **pyroclastic flows** of June 1997. Quite simply, the dome exploded. Then it grew again – and exploded again – in a continually repeating pattern which is characteristic of these volcanic domes.

By August 1997, two-thirds of the 104 square kilometre (40 square mile) island of Monserrat were left completely uninhabitable. Lava flows, ash and volcanic **pumice** stone smothered the natural vegetation and swamped the town.

Soufriere means 'sulphurous', and sulphur is a gas that rises from active volcanoes. The Soufriere Hills on Montserrat are a cluster of volcanic domes, some of which formed over three million years ago. The new dome formed by the recent volcano now rises more than 200 metres (about 660 feet) from the ground, and over 1000 metres (about 3300 feet) above sea level.

The political fallout

Natural disasters often reveal the deeper political problems of a country that have been simmering under the surface for a long time. This was true of Montserrat. Some of the islanders wanted to settle in Britain and be granted full British citizenship, which they had never had. They also wanted better compensation for the loss of their homes, livelihoods and farms than the government was offering. They wanted more than just £2500 (US$4000) for each adult and £625 (US$1000) for each child, which is all that they were being offered. These and other problems led to the resignation of the island's chief minister.

Hitting the headlines

When the first wisps of smoke spiralled into the air on the island, newspapers and television networks throughout the Caribbean realized what it could lead to. Nearby, the United States, too, took a keen interest in developments, and there was quite detailed coverage from its major network, CNN.

But thousands of kilometres away, in mainland Britain, most of the media did not report the danger until the first explosions led to the **evacuation** of the island. Mainland Britain has no experience of volcano disaster and it was difficult for the media and the nation to understand the scale of the problem.

Volcano notes

Satellite communications and the Internet have made news instantly available. This is a quote from the Governor of Montserrat, when the capital city was hit by an eruption. His words were quickly broadcast around the world:

> *It's a huge fan-shape of destruction. Most buildings are either burned out or covered in debris. Ash deposits are up to four feet thick … We haven't used the city for so long now …*

Powerful nations

Volcanic activity in the United States, Japan and Italy gets extensive news coverage. It also arouses a lot of media interest from the rest of the world. This is partly because these powerful nations are carefully watched – many reporters are sent to cover their stories.

The United States, Japan and Italy have invested heavily in predicting volcanoes and creating warning systems. They have trained many **vulcanologists** too. This means that there is a huge wealth of scientific information and knowledge for the rest of the world to share.

In times of trouble other nations call upon the aid of vulcanologists from the US, Japan and Italy. This helps to draw media interest from other parts of the world and raise awareness of what small islands like Montserrat face.

A photographer stayed around long enough to record the avalanche of debris and then the huge eruption that blasted a hole in Mount Saint Helen's, in the United States, in 1980. The pictures he took help us to understand how eruptions occur.

Although news coverage tends to concentrate on sensational stories – an amazing tale of rescue, or a complete failure to predict a volcanic eruption – it does put volcanoes in the spotlight. It encourages the study of volcanoes and ways of preventing human death and destruction.

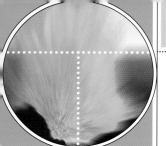

The volcano furnace

Where and how?

There are about 15 000 active volcanoes throughout the world. They occur on all continents except Australia. The greatest numbers are found in the Pacific Ring of Fire – chains of volcanoes strung around the Pacific Basin, including Japan, Indonesia and the Philippines. Some of these lie in wait, ready to explode at any moment, while others hiss and spit all the time. Mostly, volcanoes can be found above deep trenches in the Earth's crust.

Beneath the Earth's crust lies the **mantle** – a layer of stiff but sticky, unstable rock. Beneath the mantle lies the hot core at the centre of the Earth. It is thought that the high temperatures found here can travel to the mantle. This makes the soft rock swell and rise as **magma**. It presses against the cold crust, which cools the magma so it shrinks and sinks again. Scientists believe that the continual rise and fall of the mantle is what breaks the crumbly crust into great expanses of land, known as **tectonic plates**. The huge plates of land collide into each other or pull apart from each other as they are moved by the mantle.

The volcano rises

Volcanoes are formed as the result of tremendous pressures forcing magma through the Earth's crust. Many of them involve activity along the fringes of tectonic plates. Scientists have so far found four main ways in which volcanoes are formed.

1   Some edges of the tectonic plates push together (see the diagram on page 13). The thicker, heavier edge of crust is pushed below the thinner, lighter edge. This is called the **subduction zone**. The tip of the dipping crust gets hotter and melts and becomes magma. Then the hot magma swells and rises and pushes up against the crust, bursting through its cracks and erupting into volcanoes.

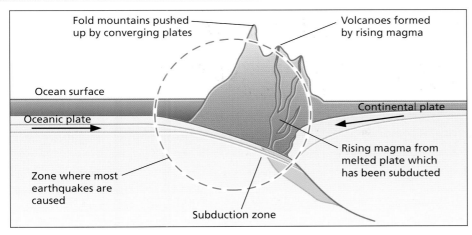

Fold mountains pushed up by converging plates

Volcanoes formed by rising magma

Ocean surface

Continental plate

Oceanic plate

Rising magma from melted plate which has been subducted

Zone where most earthquakes are caused

Subduction zone

In a subduction zone the heavier tectonic plate is pushed down underneath the lighter plate. Volcanoes form directly above the point where the subducted plate is melted and becomes magma.

2 Volcanoes can also form when sections of the tectonic plates slip and slide against each other. This causes friction, which creates heat, helping to melt the crust into magma. The magma rises like a huge blob of oil in water, forming a pool inside the crust (see pages 14-15). This is called a **magma chamber**, and it lies in wait, ready to fuel the volcano when underground pressure makes it erupt.

3 Most volcanoes occur under the sea. They form when plates pull apart, allowing magma to rise up towards the Earth's crust. This not only causes eruptions but also creates more crust along the edges of the plates, especially along cracks in the ocean floor. The movement of these cracks is called **sea-floor spreading**.

4 Volcanoes can also occur well away from the edges of tectonic plates, right in the middle of the plates themselves. They form over **hotspots** – areas where heat rises straight from the Earth's core, making magma rise and swell through the crust.

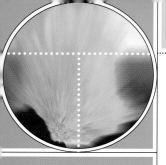

Inside a volcano

The Earth is far too deep and hot for **vulcanologists** to explore properly. The knowledge we have is gained by studying volcanic rocks and features on the Earth's surface, looking at the Sun, and studying other planets.

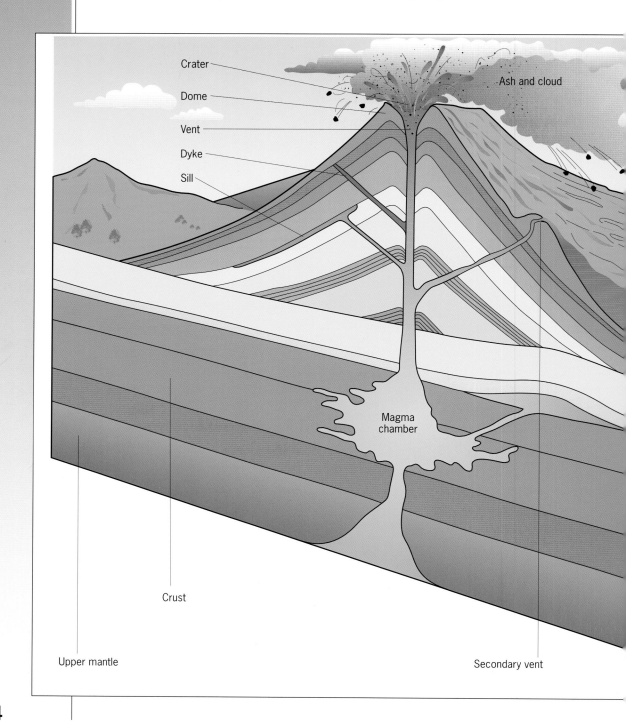

Crater
Dome
Vent
Dyke
Sill
Ash and cloud
Magma chamber
Crust
Upper mantle
Secondary vent

This diagram shows several types of volcanic landscape. In real life, these would not all be found together, but several formations can occur within the same area, or quite close to one another. We shall see more about how each of these features occurs on pages 16-21.

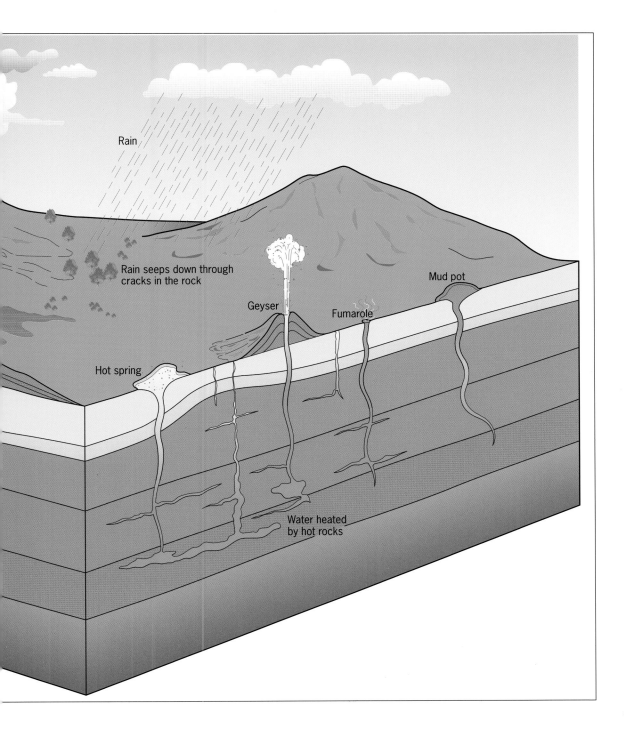

Rain

Rain seeps down through cracks in the rock

Geyser

Fumarole

Mud pot

Hot spring

Water heated by hot rocks

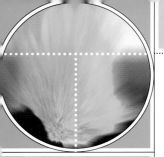

Making volcano shapes

When **vulcanologists** look at a volcanic landscape they can tell the types of eruption that have occurred, and the kinds of rock that make the shapes they can see. They also have a good idea of how a further explosion would take place and the kind of damage it might do.

Explosive ingredients

As **lava** explodes into the air or creeps along the ground, it reforms into different types of rock to create a variety of volcanic landscapes. There are three main forms (they are explained in the Volcano notes box). They can vary according to the different ingredients within the lava, the type of explosion, whether it is weak or strong and how long it lasts. Continual eruptions will regularly add material to the volcano, building up its shape. Rare eruptions will leave the volcano resting, but its shape will change over time as rain and wind **erode** it. Sometimes, a volcanic landscape will include more than one type of volcano.

In 1973, on the island of Heimeay in Iceland, thick, slow-moving lava smothered part of the town of Vestmannaeyjar. Then it flowed into the sea, creating new land.

Lava rock is made up of different kinds of silicate. This is a combination of **silicon** – a chemical **element** that appears as crystals or powder – oxygen and **minerals**. There are three main types of lava. Each explodes in a different way and gives different shapes to the landscape. The more silicon the rock contains, the harder and stickier – or **viscous** – it is. When it erupts, it explodes with great force. The runnier lavas are fast-flowing.

Volcano notes

- **Basalt** is a very runny lava, which erupts often but gently. It contains less than 55 per cent silicon. When basalt lava hardens it forms **cinder cones** and **shield volcanoes**.

- **Andesite** is a steadily-flowing lava. It contains 55–70 per cent silicon. Layers of hardened andesite lava and ash form **composite volcanoes**. These are usually very regular in shape, with slopes of about 45°.

- **Rhyolite** is very viscous (sticky). It contains over 70 per cent silicon. Rhyolite lava flows quite slowly and builds up into steep-sided domes and **calderas**, which are the remains of volcanic cones that have collapsed or exploded.

The directions taken by the lava flows are often impossible to predict. Some are very disruptive, such as this one which has completely blocked a road in Hawaii.

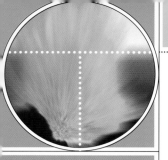

Erratic eruptions

The shape of a volcanic landscape depends on the type of eruption that takes place, and how long it lasts. This is very variable – ranging from hours to years!

Strombolian eruptions throw out **basaltic** and **andesitic** cinder and bomb **lavas** in tall, sparkling fountains, like cascading fireworks. When erupted material lands they form **cinder cones**.

Plinian eruptions shoot funnels of hot ash and gases high up into the air. The ashes and gases can reach 50 kilometres (about 30 miles) into the sky, and can get blown right around the world (see page 24).

Hawaiian eruptions can softly spray sheets of gas and red hot balls of lava into the air through long cracks and **vents** in the ground. When the balls fall back to the ground, they join together in fast-flowing streams that slither down the sides of the volcano.

Icelandic eruptions are quite calm. Lava oozes gently out of long, deep cracks in the surface.

Vesuvian eruptions are massive explosions, often from volcanoes that have been quite quiet for hundreds of years. **Magma** and gas build up behind a hardened lava plug and erupt violently into the air, forming billowing clouds that shower ash far and wide.

Under the Earth

We cannot see all types of volcanic eruption because not all of it is occurs above the Earth's surface. Some activity occurs quietly and slowly beneath layers of rock. Magma seeps upwards into the Earth's crust and eventually solidifies. It can only be revealed when these layers have been **eroded** by wind and rain. The diagrams on page 19 show some of the features which underground volcanic activity can create.

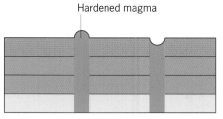

Hardened magma

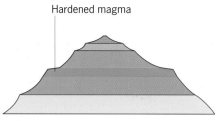

Hardened magma

Dykes are formed when magma forces its way up through vertical cracks in layers of rock. As the magma solidifies it leaves a thin sheet or wall of rock, parting the layers like a wedge.

Sills are created by lava forcing its way between horizontal layers of rock. As it solidifies it makes its own layer.

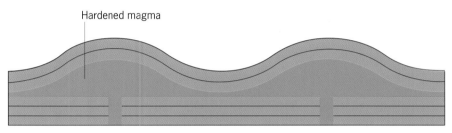

Hardened magma

Laccoliths form as lava works its way between layers of rock. It forms a swelling, pushing the upper layer into a mound.

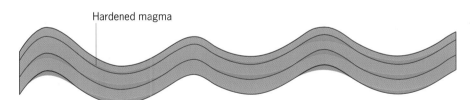

Hardened magma

Phacoliths are small rolling waves of rock and lava, like double-decker sandwiches.

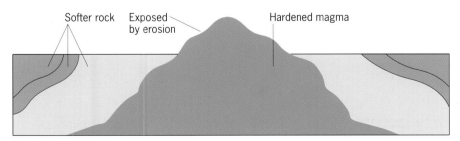

Softer rock   Exposed by erosion   Hardened magma

Batholiths are like laccoliths, only larger. You can see what happens when the layers above the batholith are eroded. The batholith itself sticks out because it has hardened into a very strong **granite** rock. This erodes at a slower rate than the softer layers of rock above it.

19

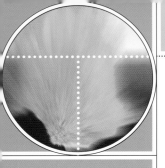

Lava land

Volcanoes make a range of shapes in the landscape.

Dome volcanoes are formed mainly from very **viscous rhyolite magma**. The sticky magma oozes up slowly and piles into a dome shape, sometimes underneath a layer of hard rock. A dome can also form after a massive explosion creates a **crater**. Then the magma creeps up into it, forming a round hill-shape. Domes can also form on the side of existing volcanoes, like the one that eventually split open on the side of Mount St Helen's in the United States (see page 11).

Caldera volcanoes are huge craters that can be 60 kilometres (nearly 40 miles) in diameter. They occur when so much rock and ash is pushed to the surface that the empty **magma chamber** collapses, leaving a huge hole.

Volcanoes produce a range of cone formations dependent on the type of **lava** erupting from them. **Composite volcanoes**, like this volcano on Komodo Island, Indonesia, are often very regular in shape.

A composite volcano is a combination of different types of lava formation. It forms a rough, rocky landscape made up of broken lava, split by countless eruptions of ash and the odd smooth lava flow. The occasional dome rock is mixed among them. Mount Fuji in Japan is a composite volcano, showing that although composites seem a bit messy, they can make quite regular and beautiful cone shapes (see page 41).

Cinder cones, or **scoria** cones, are made of small red or black **basalt** rocks full of little holes. These are made by the expansion of gases in the hot, soft lava as the volcano erupts. The rock then solidifies around the bubbles. Cinder cones have steep sides and a small crater at the top. They are the most common type of volcano and often occur in groups.

Shield volcanoes are formed by thin, runny basalt lava that flows freely and quickly along the ground, sometimes as fast as 12 kilometres per hour (7.5 miles per hour). Shield and cone formations are controlled largely by their viscosity (runniness). Shield volcanoes often have small cone volcanoes sticking up out of them. The island of Hawaii is made up largely of shield volcanoes.

This basalt lava has cooled and hardened into a smooth, shiny sheet. It is known as **pahoehoe lava**. It can spread out for many kilometres. When basalt lava cools into little rough, jagged lumps it is known as **a'a lava**. Both of these words come from the Hawaiian language.

21

Gas, acid and ash

Magma is not just soft, sticky rock – it has gas and acid, dissolved in it. Gas in runny magma flows so quickly to the surface that it does not cause a huge explosion. But some magma is thicker or more **viscous** and moves more slowly inside the deep crack or **vent**. The gas molecules dissolved in the magma have more time to expand into the space they are travelling through. This makes the magma very explosive indeed. It can sometimes spit out with such violence that it rises several kilometres into the sky, shattering into tiny particles of frothy rock or ash which are less than 2 millimetres (0.08 inches) in size. Sometimes the magma blasts through a hole in the side of the volcano, spewing out gas, acid, ash and hot rocks. This searing-hot 'soup' is known as **tephra**.

Sometimes, clouds of gas can pour out of a volcano on their own. If the gas is heavier than the air around it, it rolls silently down the side of the volcano. One night in 1986, in Cameroon, West Africa clouds of invisible, odourless carbon dioxide gas erupted through the **crater** lake, Nyos, killing 1887 people and 3000 cattle.

Volcano notes

- Acids and other chemicals found in magma include fluorine, hydrochloric acid, hydrofluoric acid, sulphur dioxide and sulphuric acid.

- Gases found in magma include ammonia, carbon dioxide, carbon monoxide, hydrochloric acid, hydrofluoric acid, sulphur dioxide and sulphuric acid. (Acids are not just liquids – they can occur in a gas form, too.)

- Problems humans and animals face when they breathe in gases and acids include **suffocation**, blood poisoning, burns inside and outside the body, lung infections and irritation of the eyes, skin, nose and throat.

Glowing and flowing

In a **Plinian** eruption, a huge, glowing, frothy cloud of tephra forces its way out of the volcano. The gas, ash and dust melt into a spray at an amazing temperature of 600°C (1048°F). If part of the volcano collapses, a thick mass of tephra rolls down the side of the volcano, masked by the cloud. This phenomenon is known as a **nuée ardente** – French for 'glowing avalanche'. It can move down a slope at 100 kilometres per hour (about 60 miles per hour) and can stretch a distance of 10 kilometres (6 miles). When this type of blast is larger and travels twice as fast it is known as a **pyroclastic flow**. This the most dangerous type of eruption.

Some volcanoes rise so high that ice and snow settle on their summits. When the volcano explodes, ash mixes with the snow and ice, turning it into a mudslide known as a **lahar**. Lahars are fast-flowing and can smother everything in their way – like this village in the Philippines.

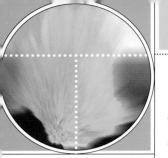

Affecting the weather

Violent, volcanic eruptions are often followed by fantastic sunsets. The Sun's rays are bent and split by the gases and ash thrown up high into the sky. It has long been believed that volcanic eruptions of gas and ash also affect the weather. In fact, millions of years ago, they caused the formation of the world's climates by creating our atmosphere.

Plinian eruptions hurl masses of gas and ash high up into the air, right up through the **troposphere** – the first layer – and into the **stratosphere**, which is the next layer. In the troposphere they screen the Sun for several days – or even weeks – often spreading for hundreds of kilometres from the volcano itself. The gases mix with water vapour in clouds and form acid rain. They can also reach 50 kilometres (about 30 miles) into the stratosphere, where the fine dust can stay for several years. The tiny particles are kept aloft by warm, rising air and can drift all the way around the Earth, filtering out the sunlight and lowering temperatures – sometimes by as much as 1° C (1.8° F).

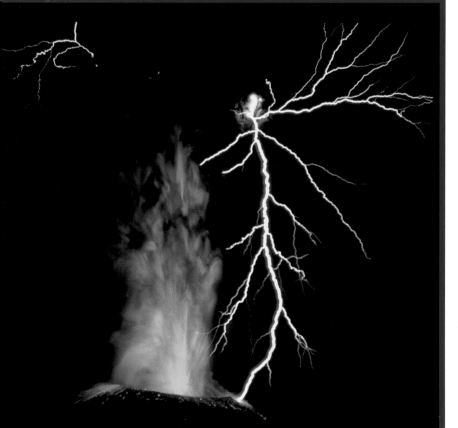

Dust, ash and gas particles can cause lightning storms that are dangerous to aircraft. Worse, the particles can clog engines. During the month after the Plinian eruption of Mount Pinatubo in the Philippines in June 1991, nine jet aircraft were forced to make emergency landings due to ash-damaged engines.

These long, sloping plains are in eastern Oregon in the United States. They are made up of layers of solidified flood **basalt**. They were formed by **hotspot** eruptions between 15.5 and 17.5 million years ago. By examining fossils in the coal-like bottom layer, we know that the area once had a warm climate, with large walnut trees, spruces and Douglas firs. In the upper layers, none of these tree fossils exist, suggesting that the eruptions cooled the climate.

Volcano notes

- On the island of Sumbawa in Indonesia, between 10 and 12 April 1815, there was a massive Plinian eruption of Mount Tambora. For two days the nearby islands were plunged into darkness. The following year, the world had no summer. In New England, USA, the 'hot' months of June to August had temperatures below freezing point. Crops were ruined by frost.

- After the eruption of Mount Pinatubo in the Philippines on 15 June 1991, an estimated 20 million tonnes of sulphuric acid, ash and water vapour exploded into the atmosphere. Satellites tracked these particles and found that by 11 July they had reached far into northern Europe and southern America. By 15 July they were all around the world. 1992 was a cool year.

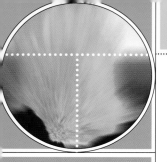

Rumbling Earth – raging waves

Volcanic activity is often closely linked with earthquakes. Volcanoes and earthquakes cause one of nature's most powerful and frightening natural disasters – the **tsunami**.

Walls of water

A tsunami is a parade of waves, some rising only 5 centimetres (2 inches) above normal levels, others rising as tall as a block of flats. They are often called tidal waves but this is misleading, as they have nothing to do with tides.

Tsunamis occur when a large mass of water is moved – usually by earthquakes but sometimes by volcanic activity. This can happen deep on the ocean floor or close to the shore. Wherever it moves, this swell of water makes waves on the surface. These become taller, faster and more powerful as they travel across the water, until they crash on a distant shore.

It seems unbelievable, but water moved on one side of the massive Pacific Ocean can cause a huge tsunami thousands of kilometres away on the other side. It all depends on how deep the water is and how wide the shoreline. Wide, open, deep shorelines usually suffer little from tsunamis. On the other hand, curved, shallow bays concentrate the strength of the tsunami, making it squeeze into a small space. This boosts the height of the wave and the speed at which it hits land. These tsunamis are killers. Boats are battered into splinters, people are completely submerged or dragged under the wave, buildings are crushed, trees are snapped in half or uprooted and debris is carried far and wide by the wall of water rushing inland.

Volcano notes

Volcanoes can displace water, causing tsunamis, by:

- a violent volcanic eruption under water
- **pyroclastic flows** that run into the sea
- landslides into the sea following a volcanic eruption on land, or around the sea bed after an underwater explosion.

It was 26 August 1883 on the island of Krakatau. A massive volcano exploded with such force that for 60 hours a cloak of ash turned day into night. Over 50 kilometres (about 30 miles) away, on the island of Java, waves reaching 40 metres (about 130 feet) swamped the coastline, killing 60 000 people. Krakakau, shown here, is still an active volcano.

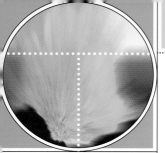

Taking the pulse

No one knows what a volcano will do next – especially if it has been **dormant** for a very long time – but **vulcanologists** have developed many ways of measuring the slight changes in an active volcano just before it erupts. Some monitoring can take place on volcanoes through 'windows'. These are holes in the solid **lava** right near the **crater**. Lava speed, temperature and gas readings can be taken in this way. **Fumaroles** on the sides of volcanoes are also used to measure how much gas is coming out.

Volcano notes

These are some of the different ways scientists can predict a volcanic eruption.

- Making **microgravity** measurements to pick up any changes in the gravity or magnetism of volcanic rock.
- Measuring weakening electrical signals that occur in the rock as a volcano is about to erupt.
- Measuring the pressure changes inside the volcano as the movement of **magma** increases.
- Detecting tilting of the Earth's surface due to the movement of magma, using tiltmeters.
- Taking **seismic** (tremor) readings – vibrations increase as the volcano is about to erupt.
- Measuring gas emissions which become more acid as an eruption is about to take place.
- Measuring higher levels of sulphur dioxide, hydrochloric acid and hydrogen fluoride often found in gas emissions just before an eruption.
- Reading the temperature of lava – it increases shortly before an eruption.
- Tracking the speed of lava flow by radar – it increases as a volcano is about to erupt.

The methods listed in the box all hold dangers for the vulcanologists who install the equipment and take the readings. A new monitoring system, called COSTEC, can be used 50 kilometres (about 30 miles) from the volcano. The equipment detects concentrations of sulphur dioxide rising into the air by measuring the amount and strength of sunlight shining through it.

Hot news

The very latest development in volcano prediction is being worked on by a scientist called Milton Garces. From the surface of the crater he measures changes in **infrasound** – wavelengths of sound that humans cannot even hear. These vibrate right from the **magma chamber**, up through the **conduit** and into the **vent**.

This is a volcano observatory at Sakurajima in Japan. Tunnels have been drilled 182 metres (600 feet) into the volcano and a sealed chamber holds equipment to measure changes in pressure, tilt and vibration. These can be analysed instantly and, if they are thought to be dangerous, the local authority and the public will immediately be alerted.

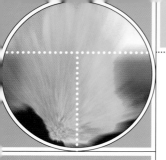

Watching water

Assessing steam

Searing hot water vapour spurts from **Plinian** eruptions and squirts more gently from **fumaroles** and **geysers**. The temperature and sulphur content of water vapour from fumaroles rises before an eruption, so monitoring them can be a useful volcano prediction tool. It does not work all the time, but it certainly gave a life-saving warning in Iceland in 1961, before the Askja eruption.

A number of scientists also use geysers to help predict earthquakes. Some geysers, such as Old Faithful in the United States, erupt at very regular intervals. If their pattern changes, it is an early sign that the ground underneath is moving. Earth tremors and volcanic activity can also cause one of the greatest threats to human life – **tsunamis**. How are these predicted?

How can you stop a tsunami? It isn't easy, but Japan has led the way in building breakwaters – barriers that break up the waves as they hit the shore – and series of concrete walls to protect coastal communities.

Setting up systems

Hawaii is a **hotspot** – it lies where earthquakes rumble and volcanoes fume. Its movements cause tsunamis elsewhere in the Pacific Ocean, but it is also affected by tremors and eruptions from other parts of the ocean. It is for this reason that in 1946 the United States' National Oceanographic and Atmospheric Administration chose Hawaii to set up a warning system now known as the Pacific Tsunami Warning System (PTWS). **Seismic** and tide stations monitor the Pacific Basin from all the main harbours in the region. Large tremors will set off a tsunami watch. Even a small rise in the normal level of seawater will trigger an automatic response.

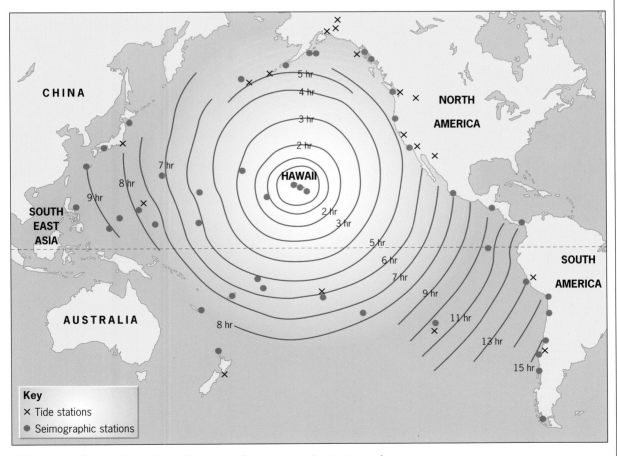

This map shows how long it takes for tsunamis to travel from Hawaii across the Pacific. It also shows where tide stations and seismographic stations have been set up.

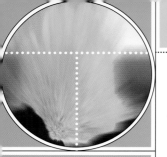

Preventing the damage

The only way to prevent volcanic disasters is to stop people living near them, but in a crowded world this is impossible. So good monitoring systems and early **evacuation** are the only practical ways of reducing the number of deaths. Attempts have been made to build barriers around **craters**. These redirect **lava** and **lahar** flows rather than stop them. Also, water is piped from crater lakes so that eruptions do not turn into lahars.

Volcano notes

The Japanese government has taken some measures to protect the people of the city of Sakurajima.

- Concrete channels and dams have been built to divert lahars.
- An observatory has been built (see page 29).
- Concrete shelters have been built along the roadsides.
- Emergency evacuation practice takes place every year.
- Education informs people about the risks of eruptions.

Vestmannaeyjar is an important fishing port off the coast of Iceland. In 1973 a lava flow threatened to run into the sea, closing off the harbour. For ten months firefighters and fishermen attacked the lava with jets of water pumped from the sea.

Rich and poor

Why did 2000 people die in the 1982 eruption of El Chichon in New Mexico? And why were 25 000 killed by a lahar in Nevado del Ruiz, Colombia, in 1985? The technology to monitor these volcanoes existed. People could have been evacuated, but they died because their governments could not afford to buy the equipment and set up monitoring stations or emergency shelters. Many such countries spend a lot of their income paying back loans to rich nations. But after Nevado del Ruiz, Colombia built the best volcano observatory in the whole of South America.

In 1992 Mount Etna in Italy erupted. The village of Zafferana Etnea stood right in the way. A dam was built and lava channels were blasted so that the flow changed direction. Giant wire mesh and concrete plugs were also dropped into the lava to stop it flowing so fast.

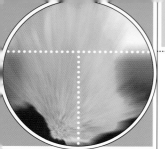

Victims of volcanoes

Monitoring and measuring equipment and modern warning systems have helped to prevent death through volcanic eruptions (see page 28) yet, in the last 100 years, the average number of people killed every year has actually increased. This is because the world's population has boomed and many people have been forced to live close to volcano hazard areas in order to make a living. So while many people have been saved through modern technology and early **evacuation**, many have also died.

Homeless

As we have seen, the people of Monserrat in the Caribbean once lived on a flourishing, fertile island. But they lived in the shadow of the volcano, which, in 1995, began to belch out tonnes of ash and **lava**. The south of the island came to a standstill, crops were destroyed and towns lost under tonnes of heavy, clogging ash. Anywhere people live on the slopes of an active volcano, they run the risk of losing their homes to lava flows, clouds of blanketing ash and mudslides.

The huge ash clouds descending on the Soufriere Hills on the island of Monserrat forced people from their homes in 1997.

Killing crops

Thick carpets of ash covering crops and pastures were once a huge problem in disaster zones, causing starvation and mass migration. People are now evacuated to other areas, they are given new land to farm and herds of animals are replaced. It is now much less likely that famine will follow eruptions.

Immediately after a disaster, governments and aid agencies are able to assess needs very quickly. Emergency food rations and clean water are rapidly brought into the disaster area. Both of these responses are made possible by modern communication networks and better road, rail and air facilities. Nevertheless, poorer parts of the world are still going to suffer more than richer ones. In poorer countries, too, many more people have to live close to danger.

In Iceland in 1783, over 9000 people starved to death after an eruption burst through a deep crack in Mount Laki, pictured here. Massive emissions of gas poisoned the grasslands and crops. Half the cattle in Iceland died, as did more than three-quarters of the sheep – the main sources of meat and clothing. Iceland still has many active volcanoes.

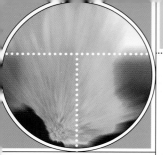

Why live in danger?

About ten per cent of the world's population live close to active volcanoes. The number in real danger is about 500 million, despite the fact that only about three per cent of all eruptions endanger lives and livelihoods. The biggest problem is not being able to predict exactly when, where and with what force eruptions will strike. None of this insecurity prevents people from living with the threat, so why do they do it?

Farming in the shadows

Most people living close to volcanoes have little choice. Farmers are attracted to volcanic slopes by the rich, well-drained soils. Some of these soils are weathered (broken-down) **lahars** or mudflows, full of **nitrogen**, which help crops and pasture grasses to grow.

On certain volcanic islands, such as the Philippines, the population is increasing at a very fast rate and farmland is becoming scarce. This has forced people to plant crops on the slopes of Mayon – an active volcano. The fertility of the soil enables a wide range of plants to be cultivated, from rice and vegetables to coconut palms. But the risks became clear in 1993, when 75 tomato farmers were killed in an eruption.

Building blocks

Volcanoes provide good, instant building materials, too. Ash can be used to make cement, while hardened **lava** and **tuff rings**, where exploded volcanic rocks around the edge of a **maar** or **crater** have become compacted into a light but solid rock wall, are cut into building blocks. In Italy and Turkey, cave houses, shops and animal shelters have actually been carved into steep tuff rocks, which keep out both the winter cold and the summer heat.

This volcano in Paricutin, Mexico, was once cornfields and sheep pasture. On 20 February 1943, a great crack opened in the ground and by the next day, a **cinder cone** 10 metres (30 feet) high rose above the fields, with hot rocks spitting from its centre. It stopped erupting nine years later, and now sits 424 metres (about 1300 feet) above ground – with thick, stifling ash spread all around.

Mount Rainier is a breathtaking volcano, only 50 kilometres (about 30 miles) away from the city of Seattle in the United States. **Vulcanologists** fear that in the event of an eruption millions of people in this area are at risk from mudflows that could sweep down the river valleys.

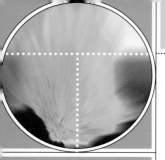

Hot water

We have seen that sprays of extremely hot water and steam can explode out of a volcano, and that when hot volcanic ash mixes with water it can cause a **lahar**. Not all volcanic water is dangerous, however. Some of it is a very useful natural energy resource – a very good reason for living on the edge.

Hot water and central heating

Bubbling hot springs, gushing **geysers**, the fine, fizzy sprays of **fumaroles** and boiling mud pools are spectacular sights. They attract scientists and tourists alike. More than this, they can be a valuable source of heat energy.

These steaming features form as searing hot volcanic rock heats the water above it, which then expands and rises to the surface as hot water or steam. For hundreds of years people have visited these springs which are believed to help with healing.

All the world's energy needs could easily be met by tapping into the layer of hot **magma** that wraps itself around the centre of the Earth, if only we could get to it! Mostly, it lies 50 kilometres (about 30 miles) below the Earth's surface and is too difficult to reach, but we can use natural sources of hot water and steam.

For nearly 100 years, geysers in Italy have been used to generate electric power. The rising steam is strong enough to turn **steam turbines**, which generate electricity. Since then, countries such as Iceland and New Zealand – and the state of California in the United States – have developed heating systems and generators from active, volcanically-heated water. This power source is known as **geothermal energy**. The buildings in Iceland's capital city, Rejkyavik, are all heated using geothermal energy.

Drilling deep

Nowadays, engineers not only tap into natural geysers, they also drill boreholes close to the raised magma source. There is always the chance that an eruption will send everything sky-high. But engineers are also experimenting with completely hardened hot magma that has not seen any volcanic activity for millions of years. In Cornwall, England, and in Los Alamos, New Mexico, USA, they are trying to drill down to this kind of hot rock. Then water can also be pumped onto it to create steam, hopefully to be used for geothermal energy. The steam can be recycled. First it is cooled and **condensed** into water droplets. Then it can be pumped down into the borehole again.

As the water around a hot spring dries up, valuable **minerals** form a crust of multicoloured crystals around the hot-water holes – bright yellow, blue, pink and green.

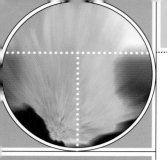

Life on Earth

Volcanoes take life – but they make life, too. Four billion years ago they started to reshape our Earth, giving out the water and gases that make life on it possible. Then out of this steamy chaos grew plants, creatures – and us.

Krakatau – a natural disaster

Krakatau – a tropical island in Indonesia – was blasted into pieces on 26 August 1883. Its once lush forest, teeming with brightly-coloured birds and insects, was smothered in ash or swamped by the sea. Three volcanoes exploded, one after another, in four huge eruptions of **pumice**, gas and ash. The island collapsed in a series of debris avalanches. In the north, two of the volcanoes, Perbuwata and Danan, completely vanished under the waves. In the south, Rakata was split into two, half of its **caldera** sliding into the sea. No living thing was spared, and darkness fell over the island for two days as ash and gas filled the skies.

An empty island. But for how long? 100 years later, Rakata was once more teeming with life. The island has provided scientists with a perfect laboratory for finding out how long it takes for a volcanic island to regain nature. How did this grey, isolated island become green again?

Within a few years, the tropical climate – over 2000 millimetres (79 inches) of rain each year, and six months of sunshine – quickly broke down the pumice and ash into fertile soil. It was ready and waiting for any plant life that made its way across the sea. About 15 kilometres (9 miles) of water lies between Rakata and the large island of Sumatra, and about 25 kilometres (16 miles) between Rakata and Java. From these two islands seeds, birds, reptiles, amphibians and mammals found their way to the volcanic wilderness.

Just one year after the eruptions a scientist found a wind-blown spider crawling across the rockscape. Large seedpods from the tall needle and pandanas trees floated across, were washed ashore and rooted into the ash. Windblown fern and moss spores and flower seeds landed on the island, flourishing under the shade of the growing forest. Snakes swam across the straits. Geckoes floated on scraps of wood and land spiders on swarms of plankton – the minutest sea plants and creatures on our Earth. Bee-eaters, woodpeckers and the Philippine glossy starling found new homes among the empty trees. Mongooses and rats swam ashore, hoping to feed on their eggs. The relationships between natural things had begun to take shape. The sea itself became a rich haven for fish, such as the large tuna. Fish-loving sea birds, like the large frigate, followed the shoals – and life had returned to Krakatau.

Volcanic activity does not necessarily destroy natural life for long. Ganung Api in Indonesia (shown here) is an active volcano but it supports a vast quantity of natural plant and animal life on its slopes.

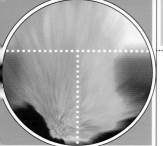

Volcanoes in history

Evidence of the most ancient volcanoes can be seen in the shapes they made on the world's landscape and the rocks and precious stones they hurled from the Earth's core. As we saw on page 25, we can also tell what happened during volcanic activity hundreds of thousands of years ago by studying **carbon layers** held in **basalt lava**. Ice samples, called **ice cores**, drilled out at the poles reveal greater levels of acid when eruptions occurred. Tree rings show poor growth during the cool climate that often follows a massive eruption. But how do we know what happened to people struck by a volcanic disaster in ancient times?

The picture shows the Italian volcano of Mount Etna (meaning 'I burn'), the oldest continually erupting volcano in Europe. It has oozed and burst 100 times in the last 4000 years and records of its eruptions date back over 2000 years.

The Plinys of Pompeii

A young writer called Pliny described the eruptions of Vesuvius, on the Bay of Naples in 79 CE – that's nearly 2000 years ago. It followed a devastating earthquake in 62 CE, which had toppled part of Pompeii, a city of 20 000 people lying in the shadows of Vesuvius. Seventeen years later rebuilding had still not been completed when, on 24 August 79 CE, massive **Plinian** eruptions exploded showering 4.13 cubic kilometres (0.99 cubic miles) of ash, **pumice** and toxic gas.

Down the mountain they roared, over Pompeii, its surrounding towns and villages, and into the sea. Pliny described the progress of the eruptions, from an innocent-looking mushroom-shaped cloud to the **pyroclastic flows** that killed 2000 people. Among tho dead were young Pliny's uncle, also called Pliny, who was a famous Roman scientist and commander of the navy. Possibly he was **suffocated** by the sulphur fumes – possibly he died from shock. Others were swamped in burning ash, **asphyxiated** by hot gas or killed by falling pillars and bricks. We know about their suffering not only because of young Pliny's descriptions, but also because their bodies were well preserved by the volcanic ash. This is the scene Pliny witnessed when the worst was over:

> '*After a while, the darkness paled into smoke or cloud, and the real daylight returned but the sun was still shining as wanly as during an eclipse. We were amazed by what we saw because everything had changed and was buried deep in ash like snow.*'

Pliny the Younger's writings are studied by both historians and **vulcanologists**. His uncle, Pliny the Elder, gave his name to the most devastating eruption there is – Plinian.

Many volcanoes have become sacred for the people living in their shadow. The Ancient Greeks and Romans believed that the active Island of Vulcano was the home of the god of fire, and this is where we get the name 'volcano'. This picture is of Mount Fuji, Japan's sacred mountain. No one knows if it is truly **extinct**.

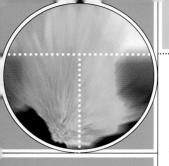

Amazing volcanoes

Volcanoes are deadly but they are amazing and fascinating, too. Here are some horrifying and intriguing facts about volcanoes.

The ten most deadly

Not all these deaths listed here were caused directly by volcanoes. Some were the result of **tsunamis** and later starvation due to crops being destroyed.

Name	Place	Year	Number of deaths
Tambora	Jambawa, Indonesia	1815	92 000
Krakatau	Krakatau, Indonesia	1883	36 500
Mont Pelée	Martinique, West Indies	1902	29 000
Nevado del Ruiz	Armero, Colombia	1985	25 000
Mount Etna	Sicily, Italy	1669	20 000
Mount Vesuvius	Bay of Naples, Italy	79 CE	20 000
Kelut	Java, Indonesia	1586	10 000
Laki	Iceland	1783	9500
Santa Maria	Guatemala, Central America	1902	6000
Kelut	Java, Indonesia	1919	5000

The next big one

Where and when will the next big eruption occur? Scientists are most worried about those **dormant** volcanoes that have kept quiet for hundreds of years. When these do erupt, they are usually the most destructive of all. This is because a plug of **magma** has often solidified inside the **conduit**, and the fluid magma and gases underneath it are highly pressurized – and highly explosive.

The East African Rift Valley is a colossal split in the African continental **tectonic plate** over 4000 kilometres (about 2500 miles) long. Through it, volcanic activity has bubbled and burst for millions of years.

Mount Vesuvius in Italy has not erupted for nearly 2000 years, yet smoulders gently from its **crater**. Wedged inside the conduit is a huge blob of solidified magma 60 metres (197 feet) wide. **Vulcanologists** cannot predict when or how an eruption might occur. Two million people live in the danger zone.

What killed the dinosaurs?

Did volcanic eruptions kill off the dinosaurs? There are many other theories – meteorites being the most popular – but there is some evidence to suggest that volcanoes could have played their part, too. Between five and ten huge explosions coincided with major mass **extinctions** of different species of dinosaur. One of these occurred 65 million years ago at the end of the Cretaceous period, when it is believed that the last dinosaurs died out. The eruption occurred in the Deccan Province in India. It is thought that about a thousand megatonnes of sulphuric acid spurted into the atmosphere, cutting out the sunlight and causing acid rain. Plants were killed by the lack of sunlight and the poisonous rain, so the dinosaurs had no food.

Glossary

a'a lava   basalt lava cooling into small, rough, jagged lumps

andesite   a steadily-flowing lava containing between 55 and 70 per cent silicon

asphyxiate   when the body cannot breathe enough oxygen to stay alive

basalt   a runny lava containing less than 55 per cent silicon

batholith   a large layer of magma that pushes up between other layers of rock and then into a dome shape

caldera   a huge crater caused by the collapse of the magma chamber

carbon layers   layers of fossilized plant and animal matter

cinder cone   a steep-sided volcano with a small crater at the top – made up of small basalt rocks (also known as scoria)

colonize   when plants and animals begin to live and then successfully breed in a particular area

composite volcano   a volcano made up of different kinds of ash and lava and the occasional dome

condense   when water vapour is cooled sufficiently to make water droplets

conduit   a channel that leads from a volcano's magma chamber to the vent

crater   the hole in the top of the volcano cone through which it erupts

delta   material deposited out into the sea to form new land

dome   a dome-shaped volcanic feature formed by sticky magma

dormant   not active, but not completely dead (extinct). A dormant volcano could become active again.

dyke   magma that forces its way through a vertical crack in layers of rock, making a vertical sheet through them

element   a chemical substance that cannot be broken down any further

erode   to wear away – usually by the action of water and materials rubbing

evacuate, evacuation   move to safety

extinct   completely dead – no longer able to come to life or become active

fumarole   a fine hot spray of steam or gas which sprays up from hot volcanic rock under the Earth's surface

geological   relating to the Earth, how it was formed and the materials of which it is made

geothermal energy   energy provided by volcanic steam or rock

geothermal vent   a crack on the sea bed through which hot magma rises

geyser   a hot water spout, like a fountain, which spurts up from hot volcanic rock under the Earth's surface

granite   very old, hard rock made by volcanic activity millions of years ago

gravity   the force from the centre of the Earth that pulls everything towards it

Hawaiian   a gentle eruption of gas and balls of lava which flows freely

hotspot   a weak area in the Earth's crust, not near a subduction zone, where magma rises up and erupts

ice core   a sample of ice from an ice cap or sheet showing its deepest layers

Icelandic   a calm, oozing eruption

infrasound   sound wavelengths that humans cannot hear – they vibrate from a volcano's magma chamber and up through the vent

insulated   protected from the extreme heat or cold, often by being wrapped in a protective material

laccolith   a layer of magma that pushes up between other layers of horizontal rock and then forms a dome shape – smaller than a batholith

lahar   a river of hot mud formed when ash mixes with water, snow or ice

lava   molten rock that oozes or flows above the Earth's surface

maar   a wide, slowly-sloping crater formed when hot magma explodes through cold water

magma   molten rock that oozes or flows beneath the Earth's surface

magma chamber   a well of magma that seeps up into the Earth's crust

mantle   a layer of soft, stiff, sticky rock that lies beneath the Earth's crust

microgravity   minute changes in the gravity and magnetism of volcanic rock

mineral   a chemical substance found in rock or the ground, often a metal

nitrogen   a chemical which acts as a fertilizer when plants' roots take it in from the soil

nuée ardente   a 'glowing avalanche' of exploded, melted volcanic ash, gas and dust

pahoehoe lava   basalt lava cooling into a hard, smoothly-flowing sheet

percolating   seeping through rock that has tiny holes in it, or cracks between it

phacolith   a small wave of magma that pushes up between other layers of rock

Plinian   an eruption that shoots out funnels of hot ash and gases high into the air

pumice   frothy, gassy lava that cools into stone with lots of tiny bubble holes

pyroclastic flow   a fast, explosive flow of melted ash, gas and dust

rhyolite magma   sticky, viscous magma containing more than 70 per cent silicon

scoria   see 'cinder cone'

sea-floor spreading   magma oozes through widening cracks along the ocean floor to create new crust

seismic   to do with the measurement of Earth tremors

seismology   the study of Earth tremors

shield volcano   a volcano in an upside-down shield shape made from runny basalt lava

silicon   a common element in rocks, that appears as crystals or powder

sill   a horizontal layer of magma that forces its way between layers of rock

steam turbine   a motor that is driven by steam, which can be used to turn an electricity generator

stratosphere   the layer of atmosphere (band of gases) just above the troposphere (see below)

Strombolian   an eruption that shoots out basaltic and andesitic cinder and bomb lavas

subduction zone   the place where one edge of a tectonic plate slips down beneath the edge of another plate

suffocation   when a person or a creature's lungs do not receive enough oxygen for the body to stay alive

tectonic plate   a huge slab of the Earth's crust which moves around on the mantle

tephra   a searing-hot 'soup' of volcanic gas, ash, acid and hot rocks

troposphere   the layer of atmosphere (band of gases) closest to the Earth

tsunami   a series of high ocean waves caused by volcanic activity or earthquakes

tuff ring   when volcanic rocks or magma have been violently ejected from the Earth, and solidify around the edges of the crater, or maar, at the centre

vent   the tunnel inside a volcano through which magma rises to erupt

Vesuvian   a very violent eruption that explodes through a hard core in the centre of the volcano

viscous   sticky

vulcanologist   a scientist who studies volcanoes

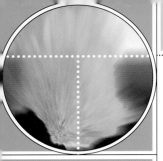

Index

active volcanoes   5, 14, 28

andesite   8, 17, 18

basalt lava   17, 18, 21, 25, 42

batholiths   19

calderas   17, 20, 40

cinder cones   17, 18, 20, 21, 37

climatic change   24, 25

composite volcanoes   17, 20, 21

craters   4, 8, 20, 27, 28, 32

dinosaurs   45

dome volcanoes   6, 8, 9, 20

dormant volcanoes   5, 6

dykes   19

earthquakes   26, 30

Earth's mantle   12

evacuation   6, 7, 32, 35

extinct volcanoes   4, 43

fumaroles   28, 30, 38

gas emissions
    18, 22, 23, 28, 29, 35, 42, 45

geothermal energy   38, 39

geysers   30, 38, 39

Hawaii   17, 21, 30, 31

Hawaiian eruptions   18

history, volcanoes in   42-3

hotspots   13, 25, 30

Iceland   16, 30, 33, 35, 38, 44

Icelandic eruptions   18

Indonesia   25, 27, 44

Italy   10, 11, 33, 36, 38, 42-3, 44

Japan   10, 11, 21, 29, 31, 32, 43

Krakatau   27, 40-1, 44

laccoliths   19

lahars   23, 32, 38

lava
    4, 5, 6, 7, 8, 9, 16, 17, 18, 19, 21,
    25, 28, 32, 33, 34, 36

loss of life
    7, 22, 27, 32, 34, 36, 43, 44

magma
    12, 13, 18, 19, 20, 22, 23, 28, 38,
    39, 44, 45

measuring and monitoring
volcanoes   28-9, 30, 32, 34

media coverage   10, 11

Mexico   37

Montserrat   6-10, 34

Mount Fuji   21, 43

Mount Pinutabo   24, 25

Mount St Helen's   11, 20

mudflows   23, 32, 34, 36, 37

nuée ardente   23

Pacific Ring of Fire   14

phacoliths   19

Philippines   23, 24, 25

Plinian eruptions
    18, 23, 24, 25, 30, 42, 43

Pompeii   42-3

predicting volcanic eruptions
    5, 28-9, 30

pyroclastic flows   7, 8, 23, 27, 43

relief operations   35

Reunion   4

rhyolite   17, 20

sea-floor spreading   13

shield volcanoes   17, 20, 21

sills   19

Strombolian eruptions   18

subduction zone   12

tectonic plates   12, 13, 45

tephra   22, 23

tsunamis   26-7, 30-1

United States of America
    10, 11, 20, 25, 37, 38

Vesuvian eruptions   18, 45

volcanic landscapes
    14-15, 16, 20-1

volcano formation   4, 12-13

volcano hazard areas   5, 36